THIS LAND CALLED AMERICA: **LOUISIANA**

CREATIVE EDUCATION

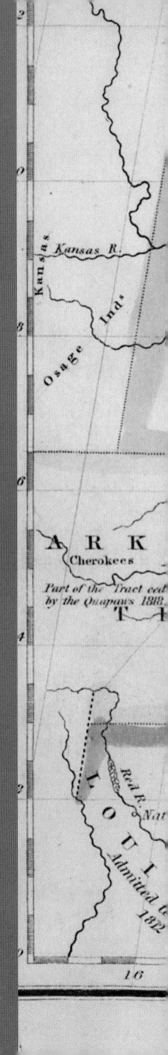

Published by Creative Education
P.O. Box 227, Mankato, Minnesota 56002
Creative Education is an imprint of The Creative Company
www.thecreativecompany.us

Book and cover design by Blue Design (www.bluedes.com)
Art direction by Rita Marshall
Printed in the United States of America

Photographs by Alamy (William Leaman), Corbis (Bettmann, Philip
Gould, Lucas Jackson/Reuters, Lake County Museum, Smiley N. Pool/
Dallas Morning News, Jim Richardson), Getty Images (After John
White, Imagno, Kean Collection, Douglas Mason, Fred Mayer, David
McNew, Michael Ochs Archives, MPI, David Muench, Panoramic Im-
ages, Andreas Pollok, H. Armstrong Roberts/Retrofile, Frank Siteman,
Mario Tama, Post Wolcott/Library of Congress)

Library of Congress Cataloging-in-Publication Data
Shofner, Shawndra.
Louisiana / by Shawndra Shofner.
p. cm. — (This land called America)
Includes bibliographical references and index.
ISBN 978-1-58341-643-3
1. Louisiana—Juvenile literature. I. Title. II. Series.
F369.3.S55 2008
976.3—dc22   2007019623

First Edition
9 8 7 6 5 4 3 2 1

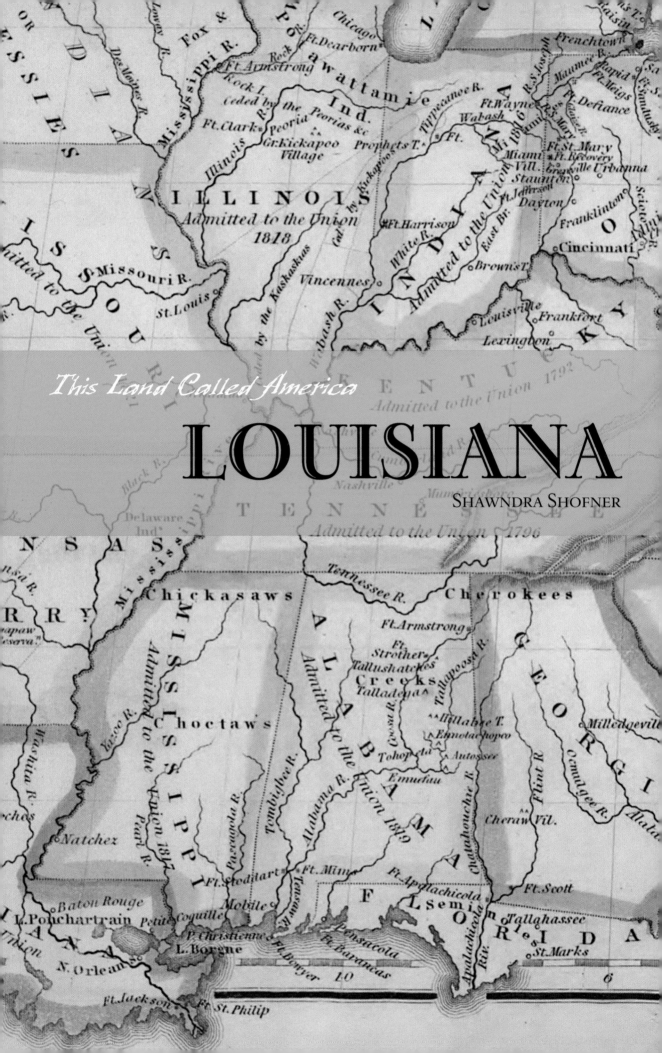

This Land Called America

LOUISIANA

Shawndra Shofner

Louisiana

SHAWNDRA SHOFNER

WHITE-APRONED COOKS STAND OUTDOORS
BEHIND POTS THAT ARE AS BIG AS BARRELS. STEAM
RISES, CARRYING WITH IT THE SCENT OF ONIONS,
CELERY, PARSLEY, AND GREEN PEPPER. THE COOKS
ADD SPICY SAUSAGE, SHRIMP, CRABS, AND OYSTERS
INTO THE BOILING BREW. STIRRING WITH A LONG
POLE, THEY SEASON IT HEAVILY WITH TABASCO
AND RED AND BLACK PEPPER. HUNDREDS OF
PEOPLE LINE UP EAGERLY TO HAVE THE LOUISIANA
GUMBO LADLED ON TOP OF THEIR RICE. EVERY
OCTOBER, AT THE ANNUAL GUMBO FESTIVAL IN
BRIDGE CITY, LOUISIANA, PEOPLE COME HUNGRY
FOR THE 2,000 GALLONS (7,571 L) OF SPICY STEW
AND A TASTE OF THE CAJUN CULTURE THAT HELPS
TO DEFINE LOUISIANA.

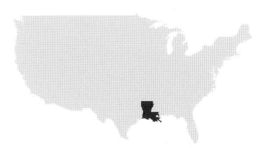

YEAR

1541 · Hernando de Soto discovers the Mississippi River.

EVENT

Louisiana Beginnings

AMERICAN INDIANS FROM SUCH TRIBES AS THE ATTAKAPA, CHITIMACHA, HOUMA, AND NATCHEZ LIVED IN LOUISIANA LONG BEFORE EUROPEANS EXPLORED THE LAND. THEY BUILT DUGOUT CANOES AND LIVED IN MUD-AND-LOG HOMES. THEY ATE BUFFALO, SHELLFISH, AND EVEN ALLIGATOR. THE ATTAKAPA MADE POTTERY AND BUILT MOUNDS TO USE FOR BURIALS AND SPECIAL CEREMONIES.

Hernando de Soto

One mound was 600 feet (183 m) long and was shaped like an alligator.

In 1541, Spanish explorer Hernando de Soto traveled to the northern part of the land that would become the state of Louisiana. He and his soldiers were looking for gold, but they did not find any. De Soto reportedly died of a fever in the Indian village of Guahoya near Ferriday, Louisiana, a year later and was buried in the Mississippi River.

In 1682, French explorer René-Robert de La Salle brought explorers and soldiers from Canada to the Gulf of Mexico. He claimed all the land west from the Mississippi River to

On his travels throughout the American Southeast, Hernando de Soto (above) witnessed American Indians' traditional ways of life (opposite).

YEAR

1682 René-Robert de La Salle claims Louisiana for King Louis XIV of France.

EVENT

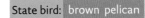

State bird: brown pelican

French king Louis XIV, who reigned from 1643 to 1715, was known as "The Sun King."

the Rocky Mountains and north from the Gulf of Mexico to Canada for France. He named the territory Louisiana after France's King Louis XIV. This large land area included the present-day state of Louisiana.

Settlers from France sailed across the ocean to the new French land in America. Many made their homes near the trading post at Natchitoches. It was established along the Red River by French-Canadian explorer Louis Juchereau de St. Denis in 1714. From the outpost, the French could trade with the nearby Natchitoches Indians and the Spanish in Mexico.

In 1718, French settlers established the city of New Orleans. The settlers planted cotton and sugar cane nearby. Their small farms soon grew into large plantations. Within a year, farmers realized that they could not do all the work themselves. They brought slaves from Africa to do the planting and harvesting for them. Settlers from Germany also came to the new land. They settled north of New Orleans along the Mississippi River in a region called the German Coast.

Spanish settlers began arriving in Louisiana after France gave the territory to Spain in 1762. Soon after, several thousand French-speaking people from eastern Canada were forced from their homes in Acadia by invading English soldiers. They migrated to southwestern Louisiana, and from them came the

YEAR

1718   New Orleans' St. Louis Cathedral, the oldest cathedral in the U.S., is built.

EVENT

During the War of 1812 (which lasted until 1815), New Orleans was an important battleground.

Cajun people, with their unique music, food, and language.

In 1800, France's emperor, Napoleon Bonaparte, took the Louisiana territory back by force. Three years later, Bonaparte sold the whole 828,000 square miles (2,144,520 sq km) of land to the United States for $15 million. The sale was known as the Louisiana Purchase, and it doubled the size of the U.S. Later, 13 states (or parts of future states) were created from the Louisiana Purchase. Land that was first called the Territory of New Orleans became the state of Louisiana in 1812.

Because of New Orleans' location along an important trade route, the Mississippi River, the English tried to take over the city in 1815. General Andrew Jackson gathered soldiers, settlers, pirates, and Chocktaw Indians to fight off the English. He even recruited slaves and offered them their freedom if they were victorious. Jackson and his troops won, securing New Orleans for America.

American politicians Robert Livingston and James Monroe (center and right) signed the Louisiana Purchase.

YEAR

1812 · The first steamboat to navigate the Mississippi River arrives at New Orleans on January 10.

EVENT

Louisiana Land

Louisiana is located in the southeastern part of the U.S. On the south, it is bordered by the Gulf of Mexico. Louisiana's 7,721-mile (12,430 km) coastline is the third-longest in the U.S. To the state's north is Arkansas. The state of Mississippi lies to the east, and Texas lies to the west.

Sugar-cane plantations along the Mississippi River flourished in 19th-century Louisiana.

Three land regions are found in Louisiana. The West Gulf Coastal Plain lies west of the Mississippi River. It stretches from Louisiana's northern border to the Gulf of Mexico. In the region, grassy swamps extend north into Louisiana's interior until prairies and rolling hills take over. The land gradually rises until it reaches its highest point at Driskill Mountain, which stands 535 feet (163 m) above the landscape. Pine and oak trees in the northern Coastal Plain and marshes in the south offer habitats for the Louisiana pine snake, Kisatchie salamander, and rare birds such as the red-cockaded woodpecker and Bachman's sparrow.

The East Gulf Coastal Plain contains Louisiana's land that is east of the Mississippi and north of Lake Pontchartrain. Hills in the northern part of the Plain give way to swampy land in the south. Longleaf pines once covered much of the East Gulf Coastal Plain. However, clearing land for farms and the need for lumber left the land bare. Many native animals such as the heelspitter mussel, ringed sawback turtle, and Louisiana black bear are now endangered or threatened. The pinewoods lily and bog flame flower are a couple of the rare plants protected here.

Two road bridges span Lake Pontchartrain, near New Orleans in southeastern Louisiana.

YEAR

1823 The first natural gas field is discovered in Louisiana.

EVENT

The southernmost part of Louisiana in the east is part of the Mississippi Plain. Oak, cypress, hickory, and elm trees grow in the soggy wetlands near the region's rivers. The rivers often flood, which makes the land even wetter. But the floodwaters also bring new, rich dirt to the land, which helps plants grow. Threatened or endangered birds, including the American swallow-tailed kite, wood thrush, and interior least tern, make this area of Louisiana home.

Freshwater lakes that were once rivers are called oxbow lakes. Many of these are found along the Mississippi. The Mississippi, Red, Ouachita, and Atchafalaya rivers have flooded so often and contain so much silt and

Louisiana's swamps contain trees and shrubs such as bald cypresses (opposite), which grow up to 120 feet (37 m) tall, and are home to such birds as the wood thrush (above).

1838   The first Mardi Gras parade is held in New Orleans.

*Sometimes levees break,
as they did during 2005's
Hurricane Katrina,
because floodwaters are
too strong.*

Levee breaking

clay that their riverbeds are higher than much of the surrounding land. This leaves the land vulnerable to flooding, because the rivers can easily spill over their banks. Almost 2,000 miles (3,220 km) of levees and other structures protect the land from flooding.

Louisiana is extremely rich in mineral resources and fossil fuels. The marshes near the coast contain deposits of salt as well as sand, stone, and clay. Large stores of petroleum and natural gas lie underground. Many oil fields are located offshore in the Gulf of Mexico and in southern and northwestern Louisiana. The state ranks second in natural gas production and third in petroleum production in the U.S.

Temperatures in Louisiana are hot in the summer and mild in the winter. The average high in July is 82 °F (28 °C). In January, temperatures hover around 50 °F (10 °C). Rainfall averages about 57 inches (145 cm) a year. Some years may have more rain as a result of hurricanes that strike the coast in late summer and early fall, such as 2005's Hurricane Katrina.

In Louisiana, selling catfish can be good business, as the fish are found in waters statewide.

YEAR

1862   The first salt mine in the Western Hemisphere is discovered on Louisiana's Avery Island.

EVENT

- 17 -

Living in Louisiana

Most Louisianans have European roots. Many are descendants of the first settlers that came from France and Spain. There are also those whose heritage is Irish, German, or Italian. Others moved to Louisiana from nearby states.

When people came from France and Spain to settle in Louisiana, they were called Creoles. The first Creoles practiced the Roman Catholic faith. They farmed on large plantations. Today, many Creoles live in and around New Orleans. French people who were forced out of Canada by the English in the 1750s were called Acadians. They built their first homes in Louisiana at Saint Martinsville. Today, Acadians are referred to as Cajuns. They live in southern Louisiana and many still speak the language of Cajun French.

The culture of African Americans has long had a strong influence on the music made in Louisiana.

American poet Henry Wadsworth Longfellow wrote a famous tale in 1847 about a group of Acadians.

Even after African Americans were freed from slavery, many continued to work in cotton fields.

Before Europeans settled in Louisiana, the area was home to American Indians. Much of their land was taken over by white settlers. Some Indians left for lands nearby. Others suffered from diseases brought by the Europeans. Still, members of the Chitimacha, Coushatta, Houma, and Tunica-Biloxi tribes can be found in Louisiana today.

A little more than one-third of the population in Louisiana is African American. Africans first came to the state as slaves for European plantation owners. A small group of free Africans lived on an island in the Gulf called Ile Brevelle. After the North won the Civil War and set the slaves free in 1865, many former slaves worked on their own farms in Louisiana or found work in city factories. Some moved to northern states.

The jazz music created by African Americans in New Orleans is also played at funeral parades.

YEAR
1867   Shrimp is first canned commercially at Grand Terre Island.
EVENT

- 20 -

The first Sugar Bowl football game is played, and New Orleans' Tulane University beats Temple University.

7450.   ON THE LEVEE, NEW ORLEANS, LA.

Shrimping boat

Because much of Louisiana is threatened by flooding, people build levees to protect the land.

People from China came to Louisiana in the 19th century. They paid for their trip to America by working on the railroads or in rice fields. People also came from Vietnam to escape the dangerous living conditions in their country during the Vietnam War of the 1960s and 1970s. Today, more than 30,000 Asian Americans live in Louisiana.

Farmers in Louisiana produce a wide variety of food products. In the north, they grow fruits, vegetables, and grains, including strawberries, potatoes, and oats. In the humid, wet, southern part of the state, farmers grow rice and sugar cane. Cotton is another common crop in Louisiana. Ranchers produce beef cattle, sheep, poultry and catfish.

Louisiana's vast stores of natural resources contribute to many industries. Forests are logged, and the wood is used for building materials and paper products. From coastal waters, fishermen catch seafood, including shrimp, oysters, and blue crabs. Salt from mines in the north-central part of the state and in the south near Belle Isle is used for seasoning food or deicing frozen roads in northern states.

Louisiana's shrimp industry was hit hard by Hurricane Katrina, which destroyed thousands of boats.

YEAR

1947   Kerr-McGee Corporation drills the first offshore commercial oil well near Morgan City.

EVENT

- 23 -

J azz music got its start in New Orleans. The music is a combination of African rhythms and European instruments. One of the most famous jazz musicians and entertainers was Louis Armstrong. He first became popular because of his great skills on the trumpet. Later, he was known as an accomplished jazz singer as well.

Well-known news analyst and reporter Cokie Roberts was born in New Orleans. Her broadcast journalism skills earned her many awards, including the Edward R. Murrow Award for her outstanding contributions to public radio. A successful author as well, her 1998 book *We Are Our Mothers' Daughters* was a national best seller.

Trumpeter Louis Armstrong (opposite) grew up learning how to play New Orleans-style jazz and later played his music in clubs (above) in cities from Chicago to New York City.

1963   For the first time, Tulane University admits black students.

Louisiana Sights

LOUISIANA'S STATE CAPITOL, WHICH WAS COMPLETED IN BATON ROUGE IN 1932, IS THE TALLEST CAPITOL IN THE U.S. THE 34-FLOOR BUILDING IS 450 FEET (137 M) HIGH. TO CARRY ALL THE LIMESTONE ROCK NEEDED TO BUILD IT, 2,500 RAIL CARS WERE USED, AND THE MARBLE CAME FROM AS FAR AWAY AS ITALY. THE 48 STEPS TO THE

building's main entrance represent each of the states that existed at the time it was built, listed in the order of their statehood. The names of Alaska and Hawaii were added to the top step when they were made states in 1959.

The Louisiana Cotton Museum, in the northeastern town of Lake Providence, showcases the history of cotton growing and explores its impact on Louisianans' way of life. The museum includes a farmhouse from the 1840s, outbuildings, and an authentic Homer Gin, Louisiana's first electric-powered cotton gin. The Homer Gin was manufactured by the Gullet Gin Company in Amite, Louisiana.

Louisiana's state capitol, with its unique steps, resembles New York's Empire State Building.

The Catahoula leopard dog is the only breed of dog native to Louisiana. It is a cross between a domesticated dog raised by the Indians of the Catahoula Lake region and one that the Spanish brought to the country in the 1500s. The dogs' short coats can be black and gray, red, or yellow. Their glassy eyes are light blue, brown, or a mixture of the two. Catahoulas are protective guard dogs and good hunters of raccoons and deer. They are sometimes taught to find cattle and hogs in swampy or heavily forested areas.

Riverboats continue to travel on the Mississippi River between New Orleans and Baton Rouge.

Salting the peppers is an early step in the process of creating McIlhenny's Tabasco sauce.

Also unique to Louisiana is the tabasco pepper. In 1868, former banker Edmund McIlhenny grew his first crop of the peppers on Avery Island and sold the first sauce made from them the following year. McIlhenny's hot, spicy Tabasco sauce is still used around the world to season food.

One of the most famous sporting events in Louisiana is the Sugar Bowl postseason college football game. The game, which draws thousands of spectators to New Orleans on New Year's Day, has been held every year (except 2006) since 1927. The state is also home to a professional football team, the New Orleans Saints, and a professional basketball team, the Hornets. Other sports include arena football leagues, minor-league baseball, and soccer.

The annual Mardi Gras celebration draws millions of people to New Orleans' historic French Quarter.

YEAR
1970   Dr. John Ochsner of New Orleans performs Louisiana's first heart transplant.
EVENT

- 28 -

Every year, millions of people come from around the world to New Orleans to experience Mardi Gras, one of the world's greatest parties. Mardi Gras is an ancient custom that originated in southern Europe and was brought to Louisiana by the French. It celebrates food and fun just before the Christian season of Lent, a time of prayer and sacrifice leading up to Easter.

Residents and visitors alike enjoy dozens of parades with up to 40 imaginative floats bearing costumed party-goers who toss colored beads, toys, and candy into the cheering crowds that line the streets. Marching bands, dance groups, and costumed characters are also part of the parades. The fun continues into the night as revelers seek out distinctive "Nawlins" music as well as Cajun and Creole food.

Louisiana's natural resources, diverse people, unique terrain, and various festivals make the state attractive to residents and visitors alike. Its strong oil and agricultural industries keep the state's economy growing. Whether at work or play, everyone can find something to do in Louisiana.

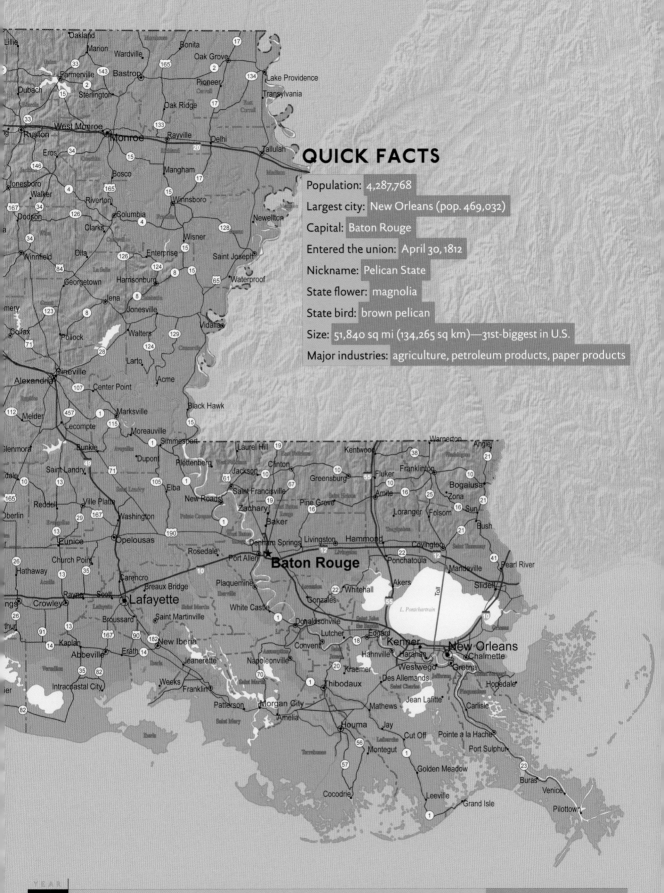

QUICK FACTS

Population: 4,287,768

Largest city: New Orleans (pop. 469,032)

Capital: Baton Rouge

Entered the union: April 30, 1812

Nickname: Pelican State

State flower: magnolia

State bird: brown pelican

Size: 51,840 sq mi (134,265 sq km)—31st-biggest in U.S.

Major industries: agriculture, petroleum products, paper products

2005 Storm surges from Hurricane Katrina flood more than 80 percent of New Orleans.

BIBLIOGRAPHY

Bockenhauer, Mark H., and Stephen F. Cunha. *Our Fifty States.* Washington: National Geographic Society, 2004.

Capstone Press Geography Department. *Louisiana (One Nation).* Mankato, Minn.: Capstone Press, 1996.

Hintz, Martin. *Louisiana.* New York: Children's Press, 1998.

Louisiana.gov. "Business in Louisiana." The Official Web Site of the State of Louisiana. http://www.doa.louisiana.gov/about_industry.htm.

Zenfell, Martha. *Insight Guide United States: On the Road.* Long Island City, NY: Langenscheidt Publishing Group, 2001.

INDEX